The history of every life is made up both of the life we lead, and the richer, more ambitious one we dream of leading, but never quite do... because we are stretched out in the bath or on the sofa, too tired or worried, too distracted or despairing.

This alternative life could be ours if only we were able to get to our desks on time, rise early enough, ask people for what we need, remember how finite existence is – or if we went to see a psychotherapist. We squander some of our best possibilities to the quiet, unheralded tragedy of *procrastination*.

Our shame at the scale of our procrastination is part of the problem. We're already so guilty about what we're not doing that the very thought of examining our errors and taking action feels unbearable. It seems as if we have procrastinated far too much to deserve a new start.

We should be less hard on ourselves – and in the process, less fatalistic about the chances of change. Procrastination is a design flaw of the human animal, not an appalling and unique personal failing. We need to consider the problem rationally, talk about it openly and learn to take small, manageable steps to attenuate its worst ills.

The goal is not to remove procrastination altogether, but to understand its roots, appreciate when it may strike and work out its hold on us, so that we can plot a nimble path around it. Having learnt the art of managing our procrastination, we'll still sometimes spend slightly too long on the sofa, but we will have opened up a major new possibility: that of eventually dying with fewer regrets •

Procrastination

How to do it well

Fear & Procrastination

We tend to account for why we procrastinate with a deeply convincing and hugely punitive explanation: we don't get down to tasks because we are lazy. We don't do what we should because we are, in essence, self-indulgent, slothful and (underneath it all) surely rather bad people.

The truth is more complicated, at once psychologically more nuanced and more worthy of sympathy. The real reason we are indolent is not so much because we are lazy as because we are scared. What we blithely call being lazy is really a symptom and consequence of anxiety.

Oddly, it tends to be very easy to get down to work on things that don't matter very much. Their lack of importance encourages our lighter, more carefree and more productive sides. We find we're done with them in no time and it doesn't even feel like work; it's closer to play.

Yet the stuff that really counts, that we need to complete because our lives may depend on it, terrifies us into inactivity. We are so scared of failure that we don't dare to make a start. At least if we leave the task untouched, we won't need to face any risk of humiliating incapacity or incompetence.

This analysis points to how we might increase our productivity. We would be advised not to remind ourselves (or get others to remind us) of how important a task may be: we know this full well already and that is precisely the problem.

What we need to do is to stress its relative un-importance in the grander scheme. So what if, in the end, we don't get the job, or lose the contract, or are thought an idiot by people we care about? It happens, and it's survivable. We mustn't ramp up the pressure; we must strive to turn the task from a horrifying ordeal to the only thing we'll know how to deal with calmly and energetically: a piece of play.

Lessening the imagined consequences of messing up liberates us to devote to a task all the energy and talent we actually possess •

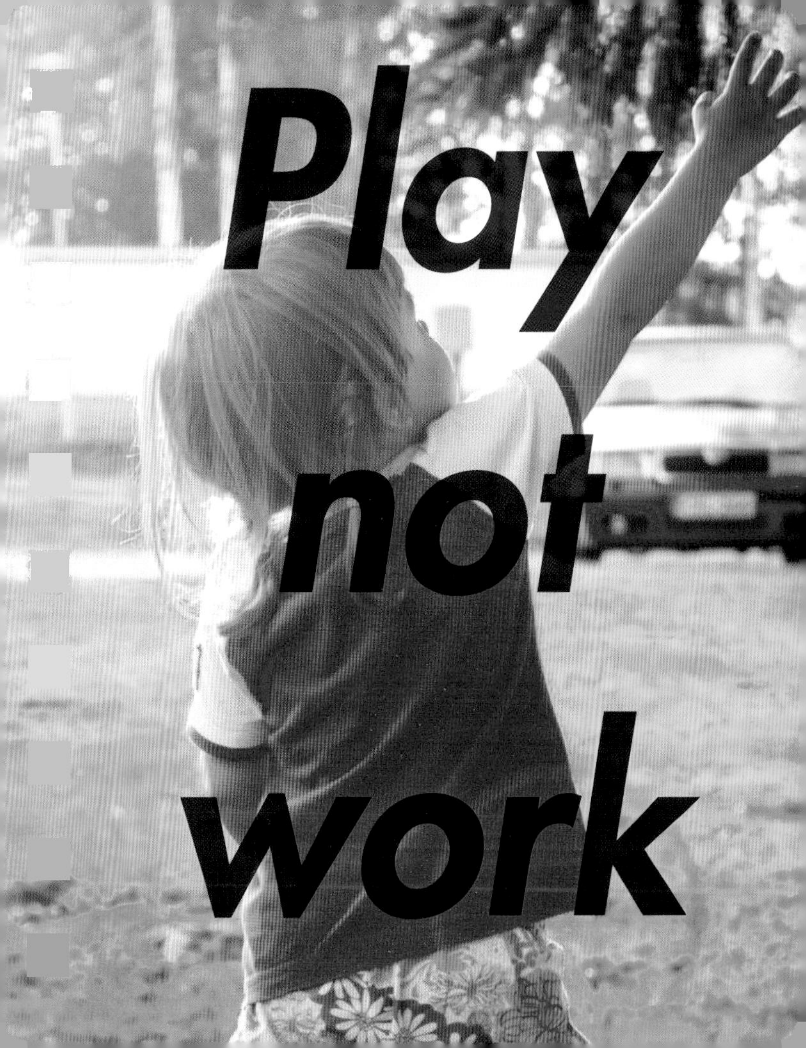

Play not work

Squeaky Hinges

In Laurence Sterne's great novel *The Life and Opinions of Tristram Shandy, Gentleman* (the first parts of which were published in 1759), there's an episode in which one of the characters reveals that in his house, there's a squeaky door hinge that has annoyed him for over ten years. That's rather a long time to leave a hinge unattended, given that it would take only a minute with some oil to correct the problem. Yet we all have such hinges in our lives.

It's a theme of great pathos: we are plagued by minor irritants that we don't get around to sorting out. We neglect to replace a light bulb, we don't refill the windscreen wiper fluid, a button is left hanging by a thread, we don't repaint a wall.

Part of the problem is that we are snobs about happiness: the issue is so small, and yet we operate with a sense that our contentment must be made up of enormous and prestigious elements (more money, a bigger house, a grand job). We leave the hinge or the button unattended because we can't imagine that our moods could be hostage to such trivial features.

But generously considered, a lot of how we feel is in fact determined by 'minor things'. We insist on a heroic view of our lives, in which great transformations are all that matter, and neglect how much – cumulatively – the small things add up.

'Small things' include not just household items, but also minor dynamics in our relationships with ourselves and others. For half a lifetime, we may neglect to discuss with a partner how their way of alluding to our mother irritates us or how much we would prefer them not to cut bread a certain way. We may spend decades avoiding a certain kind of introspection or moment of self-knowledge. We are heedless in the way we plan for happiness. The tasks we need to take on include not just the large prestigious ones around status and work; we should focus on a fair number of squeaky hinges too ●

Busy-ness

One of the odder forms that procrastination takes looks – at first sight – like its exact opposite. It happens when someone (who could be ourselves in certain moods) seems to be extremely busy. On the surface they are working very hard: at school they get their homework finished in plenty of time; around a job they plough through their allocated tasks; their home is neat and the fridge is always well stocked; the household accounts are in order; the thank-you letters get written at record speed.

But secretly there's a great deal of procrastination going on. These busy people evade a different order of undertaking: they go in for what we might call emotional procrastination. They are practically a hive of activity, yet they don't get round to working out what they really feel about a loss. They constantly delay the investigation of their own responses to an insult. They procrastinate when it comes to understanding particular feelings about a partner. They nip along to an exhibition but don't get around to thinking what the art means to them; they catch up regularly with friends but don't get round to considering what the point of a particular friendship might be.

Their busy-ness is in fact a subtle but powerful form of distraction. They are, in their own way, far lazier than someone who might have spent the afternoon gazing out of the window ●

Gazing out of the Window

We tend to reproach ourselves for gazing out of the window. You are supposed to be working, or studying, or ticking off things on your to-do list. It can seem almost the definition of wasted time. It appears to produce nothing, to serve no purpose. We equate it with boredom, distraction, futility. The act of cupping your chin in your hands near a pane of glass and letting your eyes drift in the middle distance does not normally enjoy high prestige. We don't go around saying: 'I had a great day: the high point was staring out of the window'. But maybe in a better society, that's just the sort of thing people would, at points, say to one another.

The point of staring out of a window is, paradoxically, not to find out what is going on outside. It is, rather, an exercise in discovering the contents of our own minds. It's easy to imagine we know what we think, what we feel and what's going on in our heads. But we rarely do entirely. There's a huge amount of what makes us who we are that circulates unexplored and unused. Its potential lies untapped. It is shy and doesn't emerge under the pressure of direct questioning.

Gustave Caillebotte, *Young Man at His Window*, 1875:
we should seek to bring glamour and higher status to an activity that, for centuries, has been condemned and denigrated by moralists, teachers, employers, parents – and our own guilty consciences.

If we do it right, staring out the window offers a way for us to listen out for the quieter suggestions and perspectives of our deeper selves.

Plato suggested a metaphor for the mind: our ideas are like birds fluttering around in the aviary of our brains. But in order for the birds to settle, Plato understood that we needed periods of purpose-free calm. Staring out of the window offers such an opportunity. We see the world going on: a patch of weeds is holding its own against the wind; a grey tower block looms through the drizzle. But we don't need to respond; we have no overarching intentions, and so the more tentative parts of ourselves have a chance to be heard, like the sound of church bells in the city once the traffic has died down at night.

The potential of daydreaming isn't recognised by societies obsessed with productivity. But some of our greatest insights come when we stop trying to be purposeful and instead respect the creative potential of reverie. Window daydreaming is a strategic rebellion against the excessive demands of immediate (but ultimately insignificant) pressures – in favour of the diffuse, but very serious, hard work of discovering the unexplored deep self •

Losing the Plot

James Joyce's novel *Ulysses,* published in 1922, is a cornerstone of Modernist literature, but its hold on our attention is compromised by one significant factor: the book hardly has a plot. At each stage we're conscious that a great deal is going on, but it's not at all clear how everything fits together: Joyce was trying to convey the confusion of modern existence. His novel, though widely esteemed, has a very limited audience because it rebuffs our appetite for plot. In books, we want to know why something is happening and what it's going to lead to. We like to be able to trace in simple terms the connections between causes and effects. We don't much go in for books without a plot.

This proclivity doesn't just apply to literature. In life as a whole, things can get very boring – and therefore very unproductive – when we lose sight of the plot. Often, oddly enough, we lose the plot of our own lives, and get blocked and unfruitful as a result. We may start to ask ourselves why we should be doing a particular job or why we should be putting so much effort into a relationship. We can wake up one morning and question why we have made particular commitments in love or around family. Across several years of a major project, we may lose sight of quite why what we're doing matters. We're not at all sure whether our efforts will ever amount to much, or how what we do week by week contributes to the whole.

Crucially, there may be some very good reasons to keep going; it's just that they have a habit of getting cloudy in our minds. We need regularly to step back and retrace the plot once more from the start to the present moment. We need to reorient ourselves in the trajectory of our own lives. We need to remind ourselves of the ongoing logic of what we're meant to be doing and have signed up to. We need to tell the story of our lives in a way that can keep illuminating the purpose of the small and large challenges of the days ahead •

The Procrastination of Others

Theoretically, we know that others must procrastinate. It's not as if we can possibly be the only person in the world who suffers from this particular curse. But in practice it mostly feels this way. There's a tragic, natural asymmetry of knowledge that arises because people normally only procrastinate when alone and out of sight. This means we know our own horrible habits of time-wasting and evasion from the inside. But we see only the smooth, fruitful exteriors of others.

We catch our colleagues and friends mostly in their more active and engaged moments. We don't get to see how far they may be falling short of their own ambitions. It may look as if they accomplished quite a lot – but their private experience can be of tortured frustration, in which they are acutely aware of the gap between their ambitions and their output.

We need to construct a more accurate and imaginative picture of what others must really be like. Despite the lack of evidence, we need to guess at – behind the facade of productivity that others present – the long hours when their minds must have felt stuck in first gear, unable to get going on anything serious or demanding; their failures to confront the hard questions around decisions; the things they must have abandoned because they couldn't muster the intellectual

energy to address them properly; the hours they will have spent online looking up woollen socks or holidays in Thailand.

It's still a problem that we procrastinate; but it's not a unique or even unusual problem. When we fail to get down to our tasks, we're participating in our own, painful way in the wide sorrow of the human condition ●

Perfec

Sometimes we procrastinate because of the problem of perfectionism: we're so ambitious about how something could turn out that we grow acutely nervous about our own stumbling beginnings.

Nothing seems quite right; we take a first step but are horrified by the rawness and amateurish quality on display. It's so far short of what we would ideally want it to be, we fall into despair and put our tools down. We, who like perfection so much, cannot tolerate the gap between what we have done and the standards of the mature finished products we admire.

We're like visitors to a gallery marvelling at a beautifully accomplished drawing, or a reader of a poem amazed by the graceful precision of every word on a page – by comparison with which our own efforts strike us as damning and pathetic.

To help ourselves, we should – if only in our imagin-

ionism

ations – travel to the artist's studio or look over the shoulder of the writer at their desk. The study and the studio are the places where we encounter the agony of creation before perfection has been achieved: we can see the wrecked early versions, the abandoned early drafts. We can witness the tears of frustration, the wasted mornings, the bouts of self-reproach, the multiple stages of correction and adjustment. These are, in a strange way, more precious than the polished results – because they show us how normal our imperfect efforts are and how little, really, they stand in the way of things finally working out.

We become productive when we learn to forgive ourselves the horrors of our own first drafts. And we do this primarily by taking steps to get to know the first drafts of those we most admire ●

Dublin City Gallery, The Hugh Lane:
Francis Bacon Studio

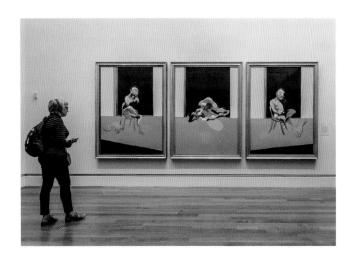

Francis Bacon, *Triptych August 1972*

A Brief History of Procrastination

We should feel sympathy for the position we occupy in time. If we were to draw up a History of Procrastination, we'd quickly see that we live in an era of acute agony around procrastination, in which it is more likely than ever that we will feel humiliated by the gap between what we have achieved and what we are striving to do. We aren't merely lazy: we have history against us.

10,000 BC

Procrastination is rare; and distraction barely exists. There is little requirement for reflection or lengthy training. Only a few people – heads of tribes and magicians – need to think. A single new idea (we could sharpen the edge of a stone so we can use it to cut things; we could store water in a pot) has currency for centuries. You can do your day's work in a few hours at most. There is little regret about the lives you have not managed to lead.

The Roman Empire, AD 100

Indolence is considered the greatest goal of life: whiling away your days at the baths and at dinner parties is the ideal (though in practice this option is, of course, open only to a tiny few). It is assumed that everyone naturally hates working – therefore slaves, peasants and serfs are kept under constant, brutal supervision. All forms of craft and trade are looked down on. Procrastination is deemed excellent: hopefully you can keep on putting off anything irksome or unpleasant for your entire life.

Lawrence Alma-Tadema, *A Favourite Custom*, 1909

York, England, thirteenth century

You are trained from infancy in your line of work; there's always a master standing nearby telling you what to do, watching you every minute. Intellectual work is confined to restating traditional ideas: no one is expected to be original. You are born into a station in life and it is almost impossible to rise or fall out of it. You don't procrastinate since so much of life is governed by ritual and tradition: every action has its allotted time, dictated by your whole society. Projects are expected to advance very slowly: it takes a few centuries to build a cathedral and no one minds too much.

London, England, mid-nineteenth century

Work of all kinds has become sacred; our toil pleases God. To be idle is a vice, to accumulate money is a great virtue. The potent demand for 'respectability' makes people spend even their leisure hours reading improving books. Everyone starts to complain that they don't have time any more. In the large cities, a frenetic spirit takes hold. A new ideology implies that everyone could restart the world from scratch every morning – or should feel bad for not doing so.

Ford Madox Brown, *Work*, started 1852 and completed 1865 (ironically, the artist procrastinated for thirteen years over finishing his homage to strenuous activity).

The contemporary world

Work is our new religion. We are the sum total of our achievements. We could always be doing something more. At the same time, possibilities for distraction have increased exponentially. The internet is necessary for almost every activity but is – by a tragic error – the richest source of distraction ever invented. The most ambitious, insightful minds on the planet strive ceaselessly to entice us towards novel ways of amusing ourselves when we should be working – opportunities for procrastination are massively multiplied and pushed widely and deeply into our lives. Employment is insecure; any failure can be fatal. There is pressure to justify our existence every day. Procrastination becomes a central secular sin, the intimate revelation of a lack of fitness for life; yet the inducements to, and opportunities for, procrastination are at an all-time high. Dentistry and plumbing are excellent, but with respect to work, we deserve genuine pity and tenderness for having the misfortune to be born into this phase of world history ●

The Distraction of the News

News got started as an urgent bulletin of facts delivered to people with a desperate need to know things: the wildebeest are at the waterhole; if you eat this kind of berry you will die; enemy troops are marshalling on the western frontier; the king's younger brother is plotting a coup. News was vital and difficult to obtain; it was the direct spur to action and a guide to wise decision-making. You needed the news to live well.

But the modern, democratic concept of news quietly forgets this. Every day, it sends out a massively expanded dossier to us – so we are informed about pretty much everything that has happened anywhere in the world in the preceding hours: a murder in a town far from where we live; an update on how the mining sector is faring in Australia; the discovery of a severed head in Tokyo; developments in a bank in France; the weather in Siberia... even though there's absolutely nothing we can or should be doing with any of this knowledge. It's merely cluttering our minds and distracting us from our true priorities.

We've inculcated the idea that it's necessary and deeply prestigious to constantly follow what's happening in the world and we've collectively provided ourselves with endless opportunities to do so. It's the ideal distraction: scanning the news still feels urgent and important, even though it has generally ceased to guide our actions and has in fact become the greatest source of mindless procrastination.

We should – when we can – dare to switch off the news and focus on a far more urgent priority: the course of our own lives •

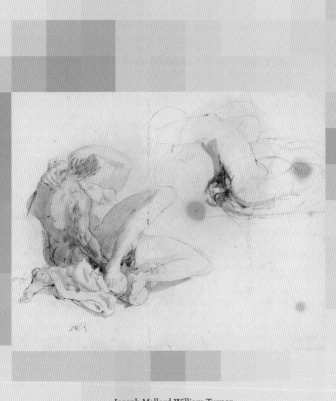

Joseph Mallord William Turner
Erotic Figure Studies: A Nymph and Satyr
c. 1805–15

The Distraction of Pornography

The nineteenth-century English painter J. M. W. Turner was celebrated for his noble-minded heroic landscapes and moody, impressionistic sketches.

But he also spent a lot of time making a vast number of more-or-less explicit pornographic drawings. When he was supposed to be painting a majestic sunset, he would often be procrastinating by pencilling a few erotic scenes. He was particularly interested in fellatio.

After Turner's death, his executor – the critic and social reformer John Ruskin – carefully hid the drawings to protect Turner's reputation as a great artist. But actually Ruskin did us a disservice. He tried to hide from the world a crucial bit of evidence: even a hugely accomplished and successful artist like Turner was plagued by a tendency towards dithering and avoidance of real work through the use of sexual imagery.

Ruskin's censorship dissuaded us from considering how common it is for our procrastination to adopt an embarrassing but not inherently shameful form: sexual fantasy. Knowledge of his images can help reduce our unhelpful self-disgust around our own sexual daydreams. It's not impressive that pornography distracts us – but it is both natural and entirely consistent with being a serious and interesting person ●

Eating

The need to eat never feels as compelling or appealing as when we have a prior need to start working. There is a particular appetite that descends at just the moment when we have to begin writing a report or complete a set of letters.

Someone who found us in the kitchen at such moments, eating a fourth chocolate biscuit or cutting another slice of lemon drizzle cake, might easily describe us as greedy. But of course, it isn't really food we are craving. We are eating because what we really want isn't available – and that is reassurance, comfort and encouragement for the challenges of getting down to work.

We don't need sweet foods, we need friendship where we can confess our darkest anxieties and be heard and forgiven; we need help in calming down about a deadline, reassured that we can withstand the very worst that may be coming our way. We need someone who can help us discover our real talents and guide us to realise our true potential.

We know, when reaching for a tube of potato chips or biting into yet another burrito, that the problem doesn't lie there. We just don't know where else to turn and there is, at least, a short-term satisfaction to be found. Our tragedy isn't our unconstrained appetite, but rather the difficulty we have in getting access to the emotional and psychological things that would nourish our anxious, procrastinating souls •

It isn't really food we are craving

Existential Angst

A boy of seven is in a toy shop with his grandmother, who is going to buy him a present. He's trying to make up his mind. He could get some special pieces of Lego, which opens a vista of the spaceship he'd be able to make. Or he could get a wooden swing bridge that he could drive his model cars across – and engineer amazing accidents with. But he can't have both.

The result of this need to choose is indecision and a degree of agony. The boy asks his grandmother if they might come back another day. Until he decides, both prospects remain possible. It's only when he actually opts for one or the other that the fatal moment will arrive. Whichever he chooses, he'll be losing the other – and the special zone of happiness it promises. It's a difficult moment. His grandmother is doing her best to please him, but he's plunged into the agony of choice: he's confronting what philosophers have called Existential Angst.

In 1843, the Danish philosopher Søren Kierkegaard (who developed the term Angst) published a book called *Either/Or*. His thesis was that life constantly forces us towards decisions: we can marry and be constrained, or be free but miss out on cosy long-term companionship; we can be sober and thoughtful but cut off from our times, or we can join in, be sociable – but know at the back of our minds that we are wasting our lives; we can seek fame and money and get very stressed, or we can opt for a quiet life but always be haunted by the idea that we're eluding our real possibilities. Kierkegaard made another observation: the difficulty of choosing means that many of us spend our lives avoiding choice, which ends up being a kind of choice all of its own. There is, in his eyes, no alternative but to face choice and the compromise that every choice entails. Procrastination isn't merely a delay; it's a symptom of not recognising that we humans have to choose and always lose out through choice.

We procrastinate, at times, in a desperate attempt to keep at bay the cruel limitations of reality. If we move city, we might have new work prospects, but we'll lose our current friends; if we devote ourselves to one specific career, other sides of our character will be neglected; if we break off a relationship, we'll be free, but we'll lose all the sweeter moments we have with this person.

If we delay choosing, all options appear to stay alive, at least as possibilities – but only for a while. Yet that is a grave illusion. We should quell our procrastination by accepting that not choosing is in itself a choice and that every choice will necessarily mean missing out on something important. We should get better and faster at making decisions, sure in the knowledge that (as Existential philosophers teach us) every decision will be in its own way slightly wrong and somewhat sad •

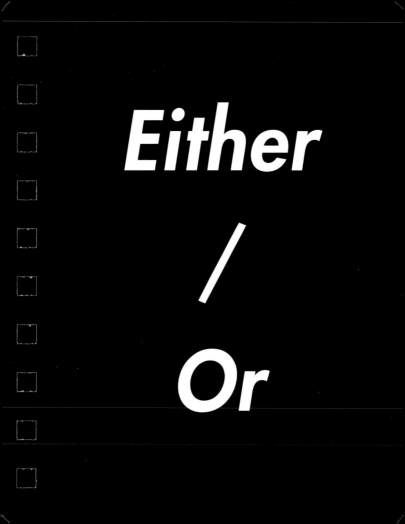

Psychoanalysis

A central idea of psychoanalysis is that the troubles of adult life often have important roots in childhood. We may have initiated a way of acting and feeling at a young age as a way of coping with what was then a very serious challenge. But we tend then to stick to this emotional pattern in later life, even when it's no longer actually needed and brings with it some considerable costs.

Around procrastination, psychoanalysis might ask a strange-sounding, but helpful, question: why might a child find it useful to fail to make headway with a project or to hold back from applying their best abilities in a concerted way? Why might a child want to delay? And by extension, why might the adult version of this child keep sabotaging their work?

The answer is that there must once have been some sense of danger associated with getting things done. Not procrastinating was a risk. Perhaps accomplishment was seen as showing off; perhaps there was a rivalrous older sibling ready to attack any signs of excellence. Maybe a fragile, competitive parent felt threatened by their own child's success or an anxious parent was panicked by the slightest sign of failure, of the kind that accomplishment demands in its early stages. In such circumstances a child could learn to sabotage their own capacities: they might feel it was too dangerous to properly concentrate and push their powers – and might stall and hold back instead.

Psychoanalysis promises us that, by becoming aware of childhood dynamics, we can liberate ourselves from the past. The rivalrous older sibling now lives in another country (and we get on with them well enough). A competitive fragile parent is now dead. There is no need to keep playing out the defensive strategies that we developed in relation to threats that no longer exist. We can dare to get down to work, take our time and succeed – without a fear that our accomplishment will threaten anyone we love •

The

Monastery

v.

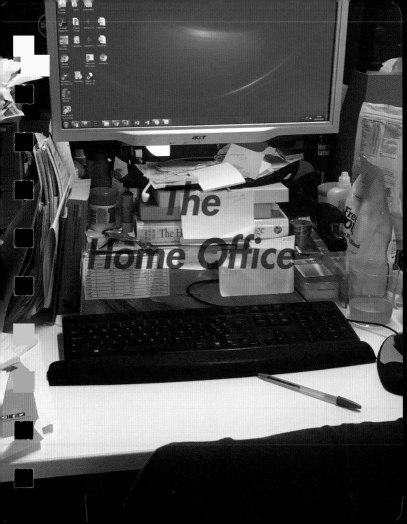

The Monastery

Monasteries were developed to help people concentrate their minds. In a sense, they were giant, beautiful machines to assist us in avoiding procrastination. They started from a usefully pessimistic assumption: we are naturally very easily drawn off course and need all the help we can get to devote ourselves to the tasks to which we are, theoretically, committed.

Monasteries carefully incorporated a range of features to assist us in avoiding procrastination. They were usually located in remote places – to keep at bay the temptations of the town. They had codes of silence – to restrict gossip. They regulated every moment of the day – to combat idleness. Monks had little or no personal money – so thoughts of shopping did not distract them. They were required to constantly meditate on death and the brevity of life – to foster a sense of urgency. They had a system of regular confession and spiritual supervision – so that time-wasting tendencies could be properly recognised and cured. The walls of the monastery were extremely thick – to avoid distracting sounds. There were pleasant walkways under covered arches – because some of our best ideas come to us when we are pacing.

The polar opposite of the monastery is the home office, a place designed to maximise distraction and incentives to sloth: no one is watching us; there is a bed and a fridge temptingly close by; we could do the laundry or repaint the bathroom or solve eighteen sudoku puzzles in a row. Or, of course, we could look up Turner's erotic images. The home office makes a flattering, but fatal, error: it assumes that we are by nature inclined to work and only need more freedom to unleash our productive potential.

Monasteries are there to remind us that, if we are to think and achieve to a high standard, we may need to make a lot of changes to our routines and the structure of our lives. We shouldn't just blame our willpower. We can blame the whole architectural and social set-up around the way we work •

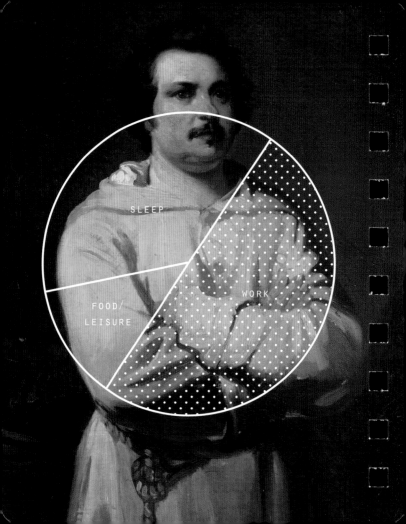

Intelligent Eccentricity

Honoré de Balzac was one of the most productive writers of the nineteenth century, turning out several novels every year for more than two decades. In order to squeeze such an achievement out of himself, he developed an exceptionally eccentric working routine. He couldn't normally write during the day, so he would sleep during the morning and again in the evening and get up around 1 am. He put on a large monastic robe with a hood and wrote through the hours of darkness – often until around eight in the morning. As he worked, he drank around fifty cups of coffee (mixed with chocolate and brandy; this had an immense effect on his brain: 'Ideas quick-march into motion like battalions of a grand army').

If he'd been forced to work under standard conditions in an office during normal business hours, or had to wear normal clothes, if he'd been forbidden from taking his special drink... he would (we can well imagine) have been deeply unproductive. Balzac's enormous output wasn't a reflection of a freakish absence of the desire to procrastinate; rather, it depended on the strategies he adopted for combating his own resistance to work. He took his procrastination very seriously and was willing to go to dramatic lengths to overcome it.

Our own productivity might be transformed if – like Balzac – we were to follow our odder instincts and properly shape our lives around the real requirements of our working temperament ●

Deadlines

It's a humbling fact about human nature that deadlines work. We are hugely dependent on someone else – a boss, a supervisor, a client, an editor or perhaps a parent – to impose a demand and threaten (in however civil a guise) to punish us for a failure to deliver on time. We might feel resentful, we might have to stay up late or make frantic efforts up to the last minute, we might curse the guardian of the deadline – but we almost certainly get the work done and are privately a bit grateful for the supervision.

Unfortunately, only a few of the important tasks in life carry deadlines. For much of what truly matters, there's no one to boss us around; no one appears to care. Our work is not expected at any particular point.

In dealing with a difficult client, a senior colleague might suggest a definite timeline and precise questions to ask. But there isn't a clear deadline around taking steps to resolve a tricky issue in a relationship. There's no one to say: 'You must have dinner with your partner tonight and ask these five questions and listen very carefully to the answers without interrupting. We'll discuss them in the morning and frame a good response.' No one has given us a deadline to work out what job we should really be doing, or how we might best resolve a conflict in our family. There are no deadlines around getting on better with your children or identifying

There are no deadlines around getting on better with your children or identifying how to be creative...

The ultimate deadline

how to be creative. And so these thorny, vital issues have a habit of getting sidelined and ignored.

Painfully – but productively – what we need to do is to create deadlines for ourselves. We need to become our own inner bosses. Furthermore, we have to tell others about our intentions and figuratively sign them up to expect a specific amount of progress from us by a particular date. We have to invite a degree of nagging from people with no prior interest in delivering it – because this is better than the alternative: wasting our lives. Finally, we need to keep the ultimate deadline always in mind, perhaps by positioning a skull or an X-ray of a cancerous pancreas prominently on our desks ●

Outwitting Procrastination

1.

One way to break paralysis around an unpleasant task is to introduce an even more unpleasant task, by comparison to which the first task starts to seem more appealing. A good way to start work on a tedious report is, therefore, to raise the spectre of a long-delayed thank-you letter or phone call to a tedious but kindly relative.

2.

Work offline as much as possible; the internet is – plainly – the enemy.

3.

Use an egg timer: work for fifteen minutes and not a moment more. If that doesn't help, try five minutes. Humiliate yourself into finding a unit of time you can stick to. It might be only a minute and a half. It often is.

4.

Use starkly accurate working titles for your efforts: 'First Rubbish Version'; 'Second Marginally Less Rubbish Version'; 'Initial Pathetic Sketch'. Don't expect it to be right for a long time. If ever.

5.

Break a task into 100 sections. Note what percentage is done. For a 1,500-word report, every sentence is pretty much 1%.

6.

Take a shower, go for a drive. We often have our best ideas when theoretically we're not supposed to be working at all. The mind is so scared of thinking, it tends to wait to let out its more valuable thoughts until we are on a break •

In Praise of Procrastination

We're so alive to the problems of procrastination that we can overlook the fact that there might be a few things to value in the condition. Precisely speaking, the word procrastination only means waiting, until tomorrow – or a more distant day. And sometimes, at least, that's a very wise and helpful thing to do.

Cherry trees, for example, procrastinate a lot. It might be five or seven years before a new tree bears fruit. An olive tree might require twelve years. But the fruit that emerges from such slow gestation bears witness to the advantages of procrastination, being rich, experienced and redolent of a succession of long summers and sharp winters.

It might be a good idea to procrastinate around having sex with someone or around choosing a career; we can be legitimately too young to drive or to leave home, to run our own business or to put up a building.

There are many important tasks we can't hurry: we can't make our children grow up quickly; we can't write a good novel too fast; we can't successfully complete psychotherapy in a few days; it can take years to assemble our ideas about how to direct an enterprise or structure a department...

Cherry trees in winter

The French painter Ingres, working in the late eighteenth and early nineteenth century, dithered for decades over some of his most impressive works. He started his painting of *Oedipus and the Sphinx* in 1808, when he was in his late twenties, but didn't complete it until 1827, by which time he was in his late forties.

In the intervening years he changed many details, he repainted some parts many times and he added extra portions of canvas to the top and the sides.

Our society is very good at honouring certain kinds of speed. We're impressed by how quickly some people can run or drive a car. But we're much less familiar with the (equally important) idea of honouring those who precisely didn't do something quickly – and did it well because they did it very slowly.

During the Second Punic War (218–201 BC), the brilliant Carthaginian general Hannibal invaded Italy and reached the walls of Rome. Fabius Maximus was appointed to lead the defence of his country, but instead of immediately giving battle, he deliberately kept out of reach of the enemy. He harried their supply lines and kept them on the move and prevented reinforcements arriving. There was minimal bloodshed. Unable to sustain his campaign, Hannibal finally withdrew from the Italian peninsula and the nation was saved. Fabius Maximus procrastinated not out of cowardice or stupidity, but because this was the wiser, more humane and more effective strategy.

By remembering the trouble impatience brings into our lives, we can gain an unexpected degree of admiration and sympathy for procrastination. It's not in principle a bad quality – it's just that we don't always use it in the right manner. It's not so much that we should try to stop procrastinating in all ways; the ideal is to direct our ability to delay to the places where this move is most useful ●

In the life of every person who gets a lot done, there are, inevitably, a great many things they have avoided.

Selective Procrastination

No one can ever be efficient in every area of their life. A so-called 'successful' person isn't someone accomplished in everything they are involved with; it's someone who has focused their energies with unusual intensity on a particular set of questions.

In the life of every person who gets a lot done, there are, inevitably, a great many things they have avoided. There are many tasks that have been put aside, and many obligations that have been neglected. Achievement mostly depends on not doing a whole host of things that, in a broad and reasonable sense, one really ought to do. The efficient person may be considered deeply lazy in some areas of life; they have been an expert at winnowing their sense of responsibility; they are good at avoiding many details in order to concentrate on just one goal.

The efficient parent may have heavily neglected the upkeep of the house. The superb accountant may have been a disaster around keeping up with the latest highbrow films and novels. The devoted entrepreneur may have evaded many tricky conversations around their relationship.

A good life doesn't require us to banish procrastination entirely; it involves making choices about where we will allow ourselves to remain inefficient, in the name of having a shot at excellence elsewhere ●

The Limits of Hard Work

The Duc de La Rochefoucauld was a seventeenth-century French aristocrat who wrote one of the greatest books of all time, the *Maxims*, in a few weeks when he was in his early fifties.

The *Maxims* is an extremely slender book, composed of only around 500 wise and charming observations, rarely longer than 100 words – for instance: 'If we had no faults we would not find so much enjoyment in seeing faults in others', or 'The world more often rewards the outward signs of merit than merit itself'.

Even more remarkably, writing the book did not cost La Rochefoucauld any great effort, as he briefly hints: 'It often happens that things come into the mind in a more finished form than could have been achieved after great study.' He wrote most of it during tea parties, and he confessed to being a very lazy person, only writing when the mood seized him; and though he never expected it to sell well, it garnered him immediate respect and enduring fame. Voltaire said it was the most important book in French literature, which still seems just about right as a verdict.

To the bourgeois imagination, this is a scandalous story: La Rochefoucauld didn't put in long hours, he didn't work very hard, and yet his little book has been selling well for more than 350 years.

[La Rochefoucauld] didn't put in long hours, he didn't work very hard, and yet his little book [Maxims] has been selling well for more than 350 years.

This violates our cult of hard work, and our firm belief that huge and constant efforts are always at the root of success. We can't bear the idea of the inspired dandy. It's become standard to hear anyone who wishes to be seen as a good person emphasising how hard they work – as if the sheer quantity of time invested will guarantee the worth of what they are, so laboriously, doing.

We've become devoted to the notion that it is only procrastination that is holding us back – and that we would succeed if only we could force ourselves to work harder.

But there is a more disturbing thought that we are thereby keeping at bay: that perhaps simply working hard isn't the decisive factor, that we might work for years and produce nothing good, or (on the other hand) sit around for decades and then – in a few weeks – do something that changes history. We fetishise the hours of labour to distract ourselves from a very awkward truth: that sheer hard work often isn't enough and that, when talent is supreme, one can get away with a lot of 'laziness' •

Renaming Procrastination

What we denigrate as procrastination might sometimes be more generously – and more accurately – renamed in very different ways.

In other words, what we do when we procrastinate is not necessarily bad; it just looks inconvenient at this precise moment and can be hard to explain to suspicious outsiders.

When it looks like we are 'wasting time', we are often at work on activities that are on the cusp of becoming, themselves, genuinely productive and admirable ●

What it looks like I am doing:
Staring out of the window

↓

How I justify this action to myself:
Giving the quieter parts of
the mind a chance to be heard
Virginia Woolf could be seen doing this from time to time

What it looks like I am doing:
Lying in bed for hours

How I justify this action to myself:
Thinking, accumulating self-knowledge
*René Descartes & Marcel Proust were both major
exponents of this*

What it looks like I am doing:
Chatting with friends

↓

How I justify this action to myself:
It's philosophy in action
Socrates, for example, didn't actually write anything

What it looks like I am doing:
Making a snack

↓

How I justify this action to myself:
Developing a new style of
cooking
Just like Elizabeth David

We should not be embarrassed by the amount of time we have wasted sitting on the sofa. It has probably taught us a lot.

There's Enough Time Left

Until quite late on in his life, the eighteenth-century German philosopher Immanuel Kant was regarded by his contemporaries as prone to wasting his time. He went to many parties, he flirted, he chatted away amiably all afternoon and evening. It wasn't until he was in his late fifties that he published his first important book: a very difficult, but highly influential, treatise on the basic structure of experience called the *Critique of Pure Reason*. Over the next decade he wrote two more major works, the *Critique of Practical Reason* (which is about ethics) and the *Critique of Judgement* (which seeks to answer the question: what is beauty?) Together they established Kant as one of the great thinkers of modern times. Yet it had all come very late indeed (life expectancy for a man of his era was forty-four).

We sometimes use the fact that we have wasted a lot of time as a reason not to begin. It seems impossible that we could be more than halfway through our lives and yet still have a chance to pull off something important: start a family, run a business, invent a machine, write a book or build a house. Tales of late achievers are therefore of particular importance to the self-hating, self-doubting procrastinating ones among us.

We should not be embarrassed by the amount of time we have wasted sitting on the sofa. It has probably taught us a lot; it has left us with a reservoir of self-disgust we can use to fire our efforts; and it has brought us fruitfully closer to that ultimate deadline to ensure that we now have the motivation to finish our real work before our time is up •

Published in 2018 by The School of Life
70 Marchmont Street, London WC1N 1AB

Copyright © The School of Life 2019

Designed and typeset by Marcia Mihotich
Printed in China by Union

A proportion of this book has appeared online at
theschooloflife.com/thebookoflife

The School of Life is a resource for helping us understand ourselves,
for improving our relationships, our careers and our social lives – as well
as for helping us find calm and get more out of our leisure hours. We do
this through creating films, workshops, books and gifts.

www.theschooloflife.com

ISBN 978-1-912891-00-9

10 9 8 7 6 5 4 3

MIX
Paper
FSC   FSC® C007323

Procrastination
How to do it well

Many of us are quiet geniuses at the art of procrastination. We tend to feel so guilty about everything we haven't done yet (and the hours frittered away as though we were immortal), we never get around to reflecting on why we delay and how we might do so less often. It seems as if we have procrastinated too much to deserve a new start.

Far from it. As this book shows, procrastination isn't a weird affliction we alone have been cursed with: it's a fascinating and solvable design flaw of the human animal.

The goal is not to remove procrastination altogether (it sometimes has things to teach us), but to understand its roots and plot a nimble path around it. This is a book about managing our procrastination, getting the most out of our afternoons on the sofa and then sometimes daring to get on with the most important tasks in our lives.

THESCHOOLOFLIFE.COM

THE
SCHOOL
OF LIFE

ISBN 978-1-912891-00-9

9 781912 891009